I Have Wrestled With the Way Clouds Weep

i have wrestled with the way clouds weep
Judy Nahum

Querencia Press – Chicago Illinois

QUERENCIA PRESS

© Copyright 2024
Judy Nahum

All Rights Reserved

No reproduction, copy or transmission of this publication may be made without written permission.
No paragraph of this publication may be reproduced, copied or transmitted save with the written permission of the author.

Any person who commits any unauthorized act in relation to this publication may be liable to criminal prosecution and civil claims for damages.

ISBN 978 1 959118 88 6

Cover Photo: dreamtwist

www.querenciapress.com

First Published in 2024

Querencia Press, LLC
Chicago IL

Printed & Bound in the United States of America

CONTENTS

Brighton Beach 9
The earth wove a casket of reeds 10
The Bookbinder 12
October 13
Migrants 14
You are what I feel...16
swinging steadfast from a tender branch 17
Aria of Space Travel Through Your Irises 20
M 23
Aria of Mourning & the Maple 24
Breakthrough 25
Practice Makes..27
of hunger & circling...28
yakamoz..29

Acknowledgements 33

Brighton Beach

In the sand, I am a dime
glinting silver glory
        drawing ratcheting gazes
of men afraid of language

        afraid the plum of me will spoil
with their words, or mine.

But they don't know the weapon
of my tongue, how it lashes

when provoked, the dog fight
in my gut, that I, too, live within
this animal kingdom
        of carnage.

I've grown accustomed to many things
besides the male gaze:

adult acne, the keen of subway rails,
        summer air damp & thick as pork fat.

Daylight, make me a forager

        a bottom feeder
with patient lungs

I will gorge myself on the ocean floor
& rise up,
        grinning

a mouth full of shells
ready to shatter into words

The earth wove a casket of reeds

In the land of sap & milkweed,
concrete chokes chlorophyll

heaving from root-strength,
blooms of hairline fractures

>Watch the granddaughter of omens
>whisper her shadow across brick

>a slate-thick sky, shelter of salix
>of wind chimes

>moth wings in her palm—

The fishermen and the trappers
did not prepare for this,

the waist-high water
flounder swimming constellations

>Watch the waves, rhythmic
>as metronome

>the fallow field, the drenched
>and dying sumac—

I am a shard of glass, scraping
blood lines across a jetty

I drink from wild honeysuckle,
suck bare fishbones

white as teeth, leave the tiny fans
of ribcage for the dogs

>Watch the mushrooms sprout
>from tongues of torn carpet—

I am an oil slick, rusted hubcap
I open every door to the shrill fever
of wind

>Make believe it is not October
>Make believe in ether, in drought

War-bound shadow scaling fences

>Make believe in the play
>of light, a mere trick of sun

>and sparrows—

The Bookbinder

Across his kitchen table
he spread out like harvested summer fruit
the leather I could choose from:
dark, supple nubucks, tans, reds,
some wrinkled like weathered hands.
These two, he gestured, *together look like
a madrone*. And with my gaze I traced
the plane connecting the chip
on his front tooth to his clear blue eyes
the color of renewal and July noons
in Ashland, the cloudless sky-blue that saw me,
age 12 and barefoot, listening for
the propeller-like whir of hummingbirds
along roadside mosaics of California poppy
and houndstongue; before I could place the name
"madrone" to those elegant trees, when they were just
"the ones with smooth trunks" whose bark peeled
off in coils like wrapping paper.
I smile, agree to the orange-brown hides
he had shown me. *You got it*, he says,
and the summertime in his eyes flashes once more
before his eyelids cast their shade and I am back
in his kitchen, writing a check and
shaking his hand.

October

Artichokes have been pulled up
wrenched from the ground, still
covered in their soil-skins

you were better with your spade—
        swift, clean
as if you'd rehearsed those candid motions
in that soldier's body

& silently, amidst jutting firs and
the folded Siskiyous, spores sifted
through the air
        through our pores
we breathed them, there, with our oxygen.

I remember the day we drove
        past Crescent City
a Jurassic wasteland swelled above us

and in our hair, there were lichens.

I placed a purple-bellied clover
        on your shoulder and you
touched me with cool hands
between the Redwoods

where shadows crept like footstep
 as if they were baby wolves
        searching for their den
the young ones, coming in from the cold.

Migrants

Mornings I lick crocuses
from pavement

pollen crystallizing like honey
in my molars.

    It is no wonder the train tracks smell so wretched—

    human beings are dying by the hundreds,

in the air and in the ash
from rogue hot plates
burning in the belly of this city.

On the bus, you are a trellis
propping up my grapevine limbs.

    I don't know which way
    to grow anymore

    so we study a map
    of the universe, imagine

    where we will plant
    our greens & our longing.

We create new etymology
of *habitat*—

    Dear stratosphere,
    have you ever held a human?

we'll learn to breathe helium
if you teach us,

we'll make propellers
of our shoulder blades.

Icarus dealt in pride
and melted wax,

but we, with fruit trees
sprouting from our skulls,

reckon with survival,
the sun's last wave of migrants.

You are what I feel

I move toward resolution like it's my breakfast,

      or a plump June supermoon—

like I've forgotten that each moment

      last summer we were picking up fragments

of perfection, piecing them together

      in 27-hour chunks, in batches

of homemade grape juice staining

      the kitchen floor, in the words we read

to each other, the odes & essays & answers

      to all the crossword clues.

resolution is a receding horizon line.

      one year later, perfection is harder

to piece together myself, and you are what I feel

      when my mouth puckers with tartness,

when the sentence comes out flawless,

      when I see the word *celestial.*

swinging steadfast from a tender branch

Pain is awakening the color of sun. I hold my pain like a wounded child and it only deepens. Today I will plod through rain to get groceries and ponder the word "might" and how my womb is a clenched pit of clotted blood, a tiny copper anchor in my cervix wrenching me down, down. But my pain is not precious. My pain deserves to be loosed. When poplar leaves tremble, they do not ache. Cottonwoods drop their boughs of hollow heartwood and something is set free. Feel the space opening from a closed cut. See the mice crawl into emptiness of rotted wood, cozy home inside decay. I am bark spliced together into armor, swinging steadfast from a tender branch.

I place forsythia branches in water and will them to bloom yellow melted butter right in the kitchen. Right in front of slowly rising skyscrapers. I will it. This is my garden among rubble. A seed pushes out chlorophyll from something brittle, encasing. A sprout's cocoon can hold life, latent, for years if conditions are not right. Dormancy is a brown exoskeleton. Dormancy is quiet under earth. It is patience for the unknown, which may or may not include light and metal mountains. I pretend the skyscrapers are mountains. That scaling one makes you rugged. I pretend the tide drags its tongue down my block, leaving my doorstep strewn with kelp. As a child, I tugged around a length of kelp at the coast, claimed it as my pet for the day. That coast, where water is a chilling smack and cliffs stand like oversized chaga mushrooms, the cusp of something holy, reverberating. That coast is far from here. The metal mountains must suffice. The tiny life that blooms in their shadows.

From above, and in my throat, sparrows. From above, I have wrestled with the way clouds weep. In dreams I take flight, soaring over city blocks, patchworked rowhouses fathoms below. In dreams, I smash windows and don't even bleed. Glass shards turn to rose petals under my fingernails. Transfiguration means to turn to cloud. To become ether. Near the water, I approach a freshly killed gull, neck broken, wings splayed. I will myself not to look away. For once to brave the birth and collapse right in front of me. That which is a cycle of frost and dust and blood. That which is the gull beating in my chest. That which is the heart, lying open in the grass, waiting for time to bathe the earth.

Aria of Space Travel Through Your Irises

I. The light is always different on San Cosme y Damian

a cobbled serpent sloping upward
from the candy pink church toward
Santa Isabela & the fruit vendors.

With closed eyes I am in a desert schoolyard,
shrieks & sandpaper air & yellow-gold haloes

under the eyelids. The light will fix itself
here, in the tiny bits of mica in the dirt,

a rock I learned to crumble as a child
into millions of mirrors.

II. Walking up the open-air stairs to apartment 3,
number 13, is ascending a sun-soaked rope

with cactus flowers tied into the cordage.
You meet me, grinning like a landed astronaut:

soft-footed, immune to the earth's pull.

III.   I learn Frangelico is not bad with Coke,
with a French kiss. With hands tracing

topography of each other's skulls.
We eat from styrofoam containers

forks breaking like our conversation
when your gaze holds me, turmoiled

& full of fractals. From the corner,
a crackling skeleton tips his hat to us,

the wet blades of grass
bending toward each other after the rain.

M

next to me on a bar stool and in front
of us, plates of peppers with huge
salt crystals. M taught me how
to savor my food, like really savor it –
she would close her eyes and pucker
up her face and chew, and she looked silly
but beautiful in that low light, her dad
was dying but here she was, eating
something delicious and showing me how.
'*Ya esta, ya esta*' she said when I told her
how hard it was holding someone else's pain,
just '*ya esta,*' that's it, the work is theirs
not yours, the work is theirs. I wanted to
kiss her that day and it didn't happen, and
it could have happened but didn't
the next day, too, when she had me over
and taught me words in Portuguese I never
remembered, when she fed me *salmorejo*
in white bowls with avocado and we ate
on her balcony overlooking Lavapiés
with slanting pink sunlight that always seemed
to ricochet through the narrow streets:
the sun, dirty spoons, the rasp of her
voice: '*ya esta, Jude, ya esta.*'

Aria of Mourning & the Maple

In winter, stained glass
becomes my bedspread,

my vocal chords, rotten
planks of wood, humming

muted dysphonia. I birth
a ghost baby & feed her

pitch from the cracked maple,
an ink stain growing

in the white of the yard.
The wind shoves

talons into my hair,
sends reindeer to pound

their hooves into my temples.
Solace is a six-letter riddle

I have crumbled to dust,
my daughter sleeping soundly,

her mouth coated with sugar.

Breakthrough

it starts like hay fever in February
& canceling my tickets to *Hedwig*.

on day 2, I'm floating above
trembling poplars & wake up in a flood
of sweat,

   a fever broken, a fall from the sky.

day 3, a mess of words throbbing
in my brain; my skull,
   inadequate casing.

day 4, dishes piled on the desk
countless takeout orders,
horizon aflame with sunset,
   a match dragged across brick.

fatigue hits like grief,
unexpected & ravaging

   confined to a queen-size square
   that starts to pucker and indent

as I research what else is anti-
inflammatory, besides turmeric.

day 7, another positive. I sleepwalk
in the dark, and also in the sun

   slow loops around the block,
   my dog at my side, pulling.

day 10, another drop squeezed,
   another infinite 15 minutes,

& yet another purple line

        detonating and soundless —
"breakthrough infection", as if the virus
made a discovery in the exhausted heap
of my body.

day 10, they say, the end of quarantine
& outside camellias blossom
& days stretch longer
& apparently omicron has peaked

but I have turned to stone
        a membrane hardened,
shutting me in—

I lift water to my lips & my whole world
        shrinks to fit in that glass,

inside that next sip.

Practice Makes

my hands raw
as I scrub sheets
      scorched by the scent of you.

before we touched,
my whole body ached
      with fluid & gratitude—

I watched the entire Columbia River
run through your fingers
as you built a house
      I imagined living in.

to walk around flush-cheeked
Home on the tongue
is to forget you are all air—

breathe you out
& you disappear.

if I were a child
I might fool myself
into loving the clouds.

of hunger & circling

after we end, I finally open
Maggie Nelson's *The Argonauts*
 my nerves catch fire—

"what if where I am is what I need?" she writes,
applying this to joy, not just pain

(something I, too, had never thought of)
which renders my throat a fistful
of clenched stones.

where I am is different from where we were
in August, encased in each other, & the dahlias;

when the sky opened its filament jaws
to let us make a home, *shehecheyanu,*

albeit temporary. how we needed that, then.

where I am now is a place of hunger
& circling, of grappling with the crosshatch
        of sunlight and heartache—

now I look for you in between the lines
of *The Argonauts*. this, of course, is futile,

but most days my mind doesn't care
to be reminded.

yakamoz

is a word that in Turkish, means
        "the reflection of moonlight on water"—

a word that actually means a phrase,
        that means the interaction of a cosmic body

with something unique to planet earth.
        in 2018, the orca whale J35 carried

her dead newborn calf with her for 17 days
        through the Salish Sea because grief

is a force like gravity, or inertia; to resist
        is to pledge allegiance

to another planet, even for a whale.
        at dusk, the other females

circled round and round and round,
        steadily illuminated by moonlight

as it shifted on the water,
        inviting *yakamoz* as the backdrop

to their collective mourning ritual.
        I want to steal this from the whales,

to call up *yakamoz* as the landscape for
        all my moments of grief. to split

open the kitchen table and find a
        lake underneath, awash in light—

or when I'm in the car and suddenly struck
        by an old pain, I want the asphalt

to flood, to make a sailboat of me,
        skimming along the watery glow.

I want the moon in one pocket
        & the ocean in the other, to roll them

between my fingers like worry beads,
        hold them close & know

that when I need them,
        I can cast them out to make *yakamoz,*

the word that actually means a phrase,
        the word that is a balm for

pain as big as a whale's.

Acknowledgements

I gratefully acknowledge the literary journals in which some of these poems originally appeared:

"*yakamoz,*" *Muleskinner Journal,* 2023.

"Brighton Beach", *Yes Poetry*, 2020.

"The earth wove a casket of reeds", *Souvenir Lit*, 2017.

"Aria of Space Travel Through Your Irises", *Axolotl*, 2015.

"Aria of Mourning and the Maple", *Axolotl*, 2015.

"The Bookbinder", *Windfall*, 2011. "October", *Windfall*, 2010.

Printed in the USA
CPSIA information can be obtained
at www.ICGtesting.com
LVHW041752041224
798187LV00008B/824